WELCOME TO THE U.S.A.
MISSISSIPPI

Written by Ann Heinrichs   Illustrated by Matt Kania
Content Adviser: Mary Beth Farrell, Instructor, University of
Southern Mississippi, Hattiesburg, Mississippi

The Child's World

Published in the United States of America by The Child's World®
PO Box 326 • Chanhassen, MN 55317-0326
800-599-READ • www.childsworld.com

Photo Credits

Cover: Kevin Fleming/Corbis; frontispiece: Richard Hamilton Smith/Corbis.

Interior: Brainstorm Creative Group/Meridian-Lauderdale County Tourism Bureau: 34; Corbis: 6 (Joseph Sohm), 13 (Danny Lehman), 14 (Kevin Fleming), 25 (Owaki – Kulla), 29 (Jim Richardson); Mississippi Development Authority/Department of Tourism: 9, 10, 17, 18, 22, 30, 33; NASA/Stennis Space Center: 21; Picture Desk/Travelsite/Global: 26.

Acknowledgments

The Child's World®: Mary Berendes, Publishing Director

Editorial Directions, Inc.: E. Russell Primm, Editorial Director; Katie Marsico, Associate Editor; Judith Shiffer, Assistant Editor; Matt Messbarger, Editorial Assistant; Susan Hindman, Copy Editor; Melissa McDaniel, Proofreader; Kevin Cunningham, Peter Garnham, Matt Messbarger, Olivia Nellums, Chris Simms, Molly Symmonds, Katherine Trickle, Carl Stephen Wender, Fact Checkers; Tim Griffin/IndexServ, Indexer; Cian Loughlin O'Day, Photo Researcher and Editor

The Design Lab: Kathleen Petelinsek, Design; Julia Goozen, Art Production

Library of Congress Cataloging-in-Publication Data
Heinrichs, Ann.
   Mississippi / by Ann Heinrichs.
      p. cm. – (Welcome to the U.S.A.)
   Includes index.
   ISBN 1-59296-446-X (library bound : alk. paper) 1. Mississippi—Juvenile literature.
I. Title.
   F341.3.H453 2006
   976.2—dc22   2005000526

Ann Heinrichs is the author of more than 100 books for children and young adults. She has also enjoyed successful careers as a children's book editor and an advertising copywriter. Ann grew up in Fort Smith, Arkansas, and lives in Chicago, Illinois.

**About the Author
Ann Heinrichs**

Matt Kania loves maps and, as a kid, dreamed of making them. In school he studied geography and cartography, and today he makes maps for a living. Matt's favorite thing about drawing maps is learning about the places they represent. Many of the maps he has created can be found in books, magazines, videos, Web sites, and public places.

**About the
Map Illustrator
Matt Kania**

On the cover: This paddle boat in Natchez travels up and down the Mississippi River.
On page one: Cotton is still an important crop in Mississippi.

OUR MISSISSIPPI TRIP

4

Are you ready to explore Mississippi? You'll be glad you came. There's so much to discover here!

You'll see shrimp boats and alligators. You'll meet blues singers and Elvis Presley. You'll pick cotton and land a space shuttle. You'll watch hot-air balloons race across the sky. And you'll eat slugburgers and sweet potato pie!

See how much there is to do? Let's not wait another minute. Just buckle up that seat belt. We're on our way!

WELCOME TO MISSISSIPPI

As you travel through Mississippi, watch for all the interesting facts along the way.

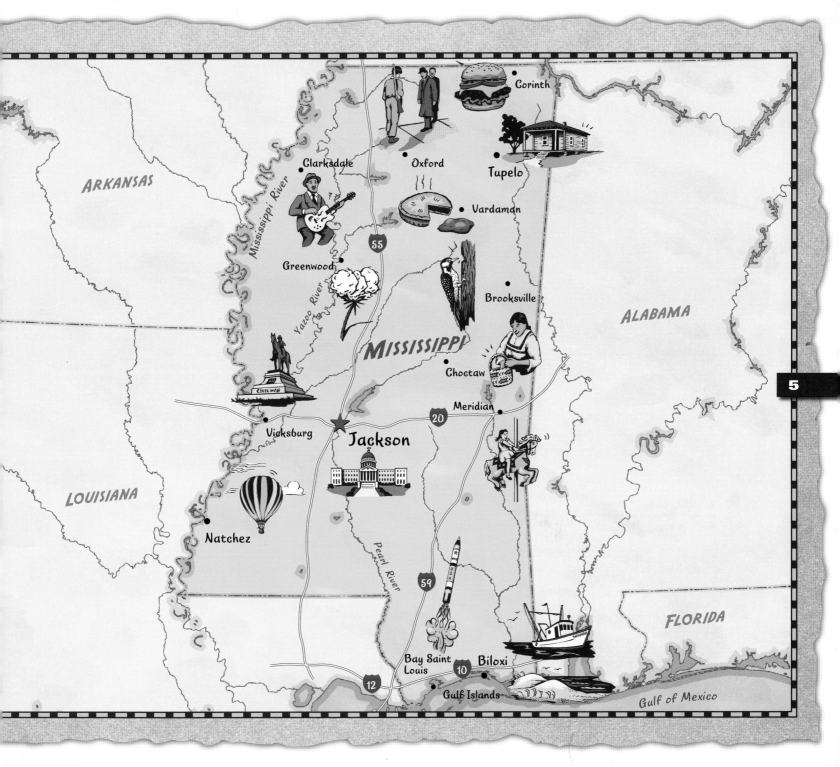

ARKANSAS

Clarksdale

Mississippi River

Greenwood

Yazoo River

CIVIL WAR

Vicksburg

Natchez

LOUISIANA

Oxford

Corinth

Tupelo

Vardaman

55

MISSISSIPPI

Brooksville

ALABAMA

Choctaw

Meridian

20

Jackson

Pearl River

59

10

12

Bay Saint Louis

Biloxi

Gulf Islands

FLORIDA

Gulf of Mexico

Wiggle your toes in the white sand. Watch a sunset over the water. Ride a bike for miles along the shore. Or jump right in for a swim. You're on Gulf Islands National Seashore!

These islands lie off Mississippi's coast. Southern Mississippi faces the Gulf of Mexico. Many islands lie offshore.

The Mississippi River is the state's major river. It runs along the whole western border. Land along the river is very fertile. This region is called the Mississippi Delta.

Rolling hills cover much of Mississippi. The Tennessee River Hills are in the northeast. In the southeast are the Pine Hills. They're sometimes called the Piney Woods.

Steamboat passengers enjoy a scenic sunset along the Mississippi Delta.

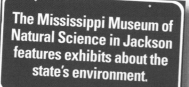

The Mississippi Museum of Natural Science in Jackson features exhibits about the state's environment.

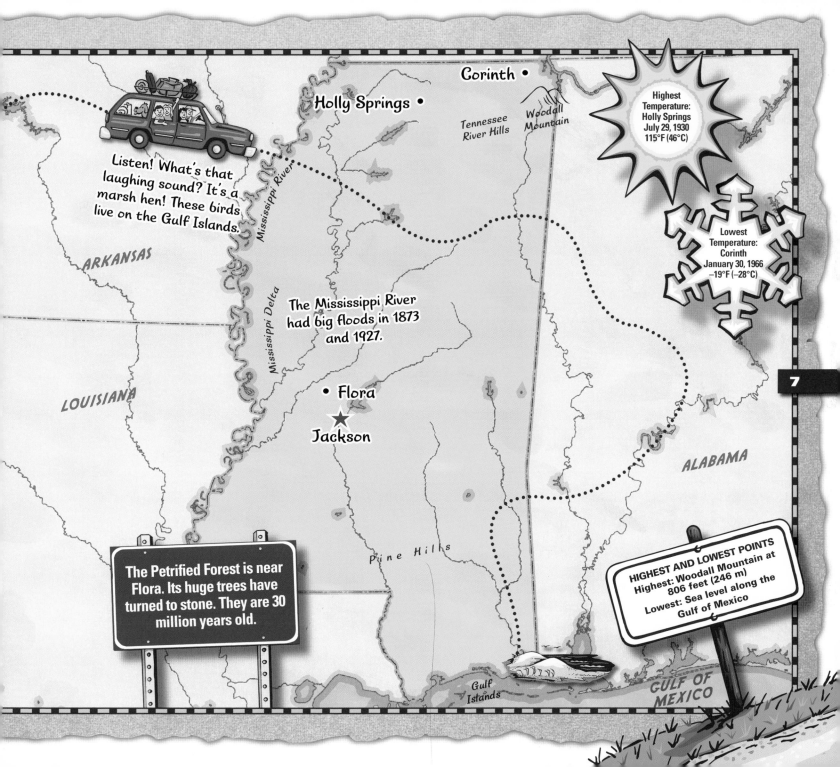

Corinth •

Holly Springs •

Tennessee River Hills

Woodall Mountain

Listen! What's that laughing sound? It's a marsh hen! These birds live on the Gulf Islands.

Highest Temperature: Holly Springs July 29, 1930 115°F (46°C)

Lowest Temperature: Corinth January 30, 1966 −19°F (−28°C)

ARKANSAS

Mississippi River

Mississippi Delta

The Mississippi River had big floods in 1873 and 1927.

7

LOUISIANA

• Flora

★ Jackson

ALABAMA

Pine Hills

The Petrified Forest is near Flora. Its huge trees have turned to stone. They are 30 million years old.

HIGHEST AND LOWEST POINTS
Highest: Woodall Mountain at 806 feet (246 m)
Lowest: Sea level along the Gulf of Mexico

Gulf Islands

GULF OF MEXICO

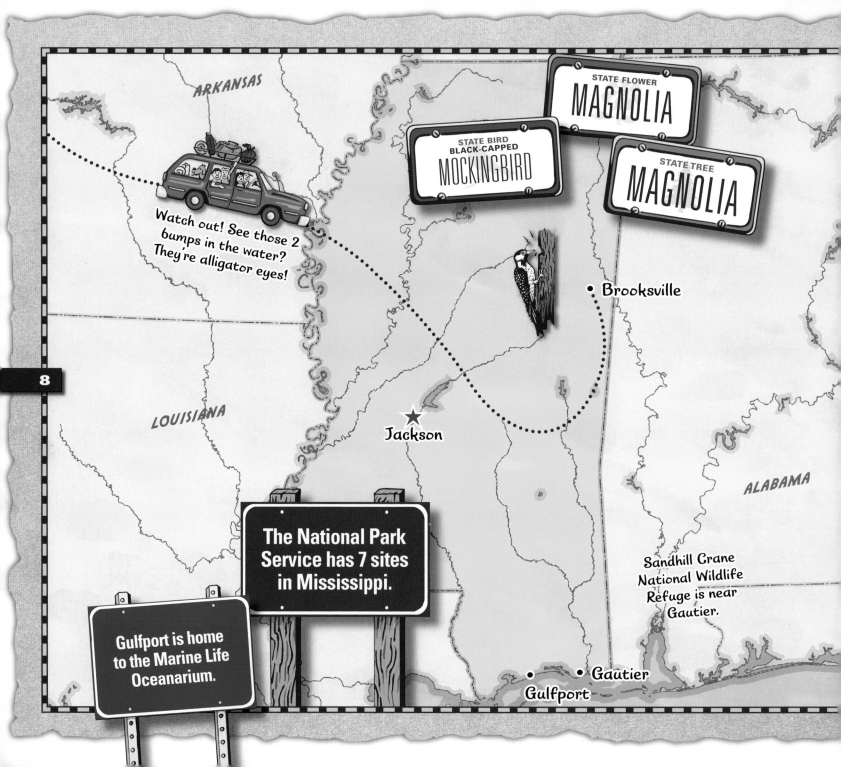

ARKANSAS

Watch out! See those 2 bumps in the water? They're alligator eyes!

STATE BIRD
BLACK-CAPPED
MOCKINGBIRD

STATE FLOWER
MAGNOLIA

STATE TREE
MAGNOLIA

• Brooksville

LOUISIANA

★ Jackson

ALABAMA

The National Park Service has 7 sites in Mississippi.

Sandhill Crane National Wildlife Refuge is near Gautier.

Gulfport is home to the Marine Life Oceanarium.

• Gautier

Gulfport

Noxubee National Wildlife Refuge near Brooksville

Bullfrogs are croaking. Wild turkeys are gobbling. Squirrels are barking. Red-cockaded woodpeckers are rapping and tapping. You're exploring Noxubee National Wildlife Refuge. It can be pretty noisy!

Lots of animals make their homes in Mississippi. Some live in forests. Others live in wetlands.

White-tailed deer live in much of the state. They have their **fawns** in early summer. Squirrels, rabbits, and raccoons are common, too.

You'll see alligators in wetland areas. Sometimes they swim or rest in the water. Their eyes stick out above the water. Then they can see what's going on!

This deer makes its home in the Mississippi wilderness.

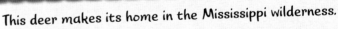

Cypress Swamp is just north of Jackson. It's a wetland where water tupelo and bald cypress trees grow.

What a colorful costume! You'll get a glimpse of Native American life in Choctaw.

Nanih Waiya in Louisville is an earthen mound. The Choctaw honor it as the birthplace of their people.

The Choctaw Indian Fair in Choctaw

Watch the dancers tell stories with their moves. Colorful feathers, beads, and fringe decorate their costumes. Then try some delicious **hominy** or **frybread.** It's the Choctaw Indian Fair!

Thousands of Native Americans once lived in Mississippi. They hunted in the forests and grew crops. They explained their history with many **legends.**

Spanish Explorer Hernando de Soto arrived in 1540. French explorers came in the 1600s and 1700s. They made settlements and began farming.

The new settlers kept wanting more Indian lands. The two groups often clashed in battle.

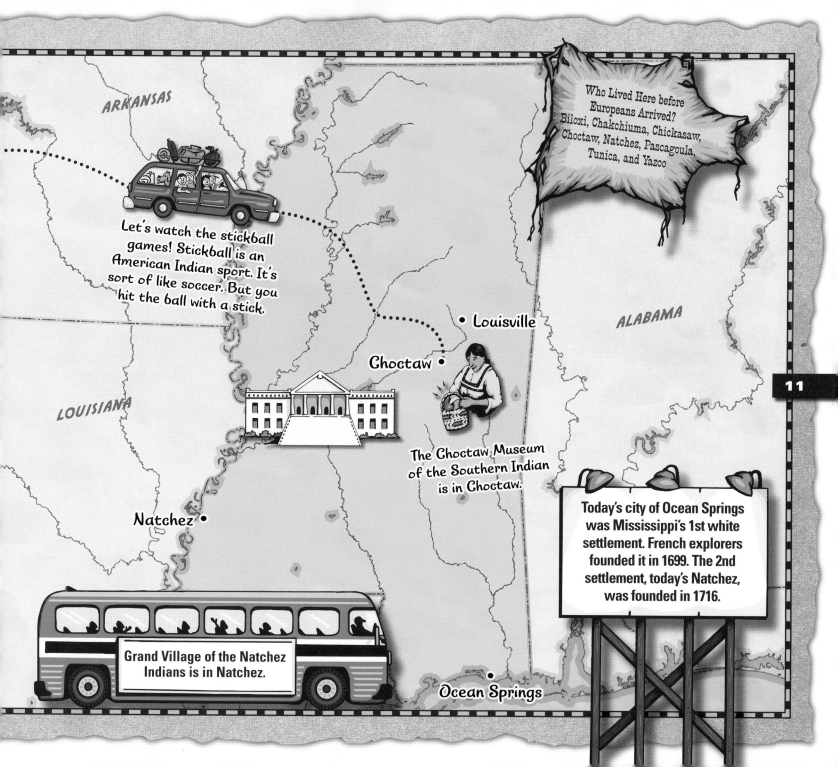

ARKANSAS

Let's watch the stickball games! Stickball is an American Indian sport. It's sort of like soccer. But you hit the ball with a stick.

LOUISIANA

Who Lived Here before Europeans Arrived? Biloxi, Chakchiuma, Chickasaw, Choctaw, Natchez, Pascagoula, Tunica, and Yazoo

ALABAMA

• Louisville

Choctaw •

The Choctaw Museum of the Southern Indian is in Choctaw.

Natchez •

Today's city of Ocean Springs was Mississippi's 1st white settlement. French explorers founded it in 1699. The 2nd settlement, today's Natchez, was founded in 1716.

Grand Village of the Natchez Indians is in Natchez.

Ocean Springs

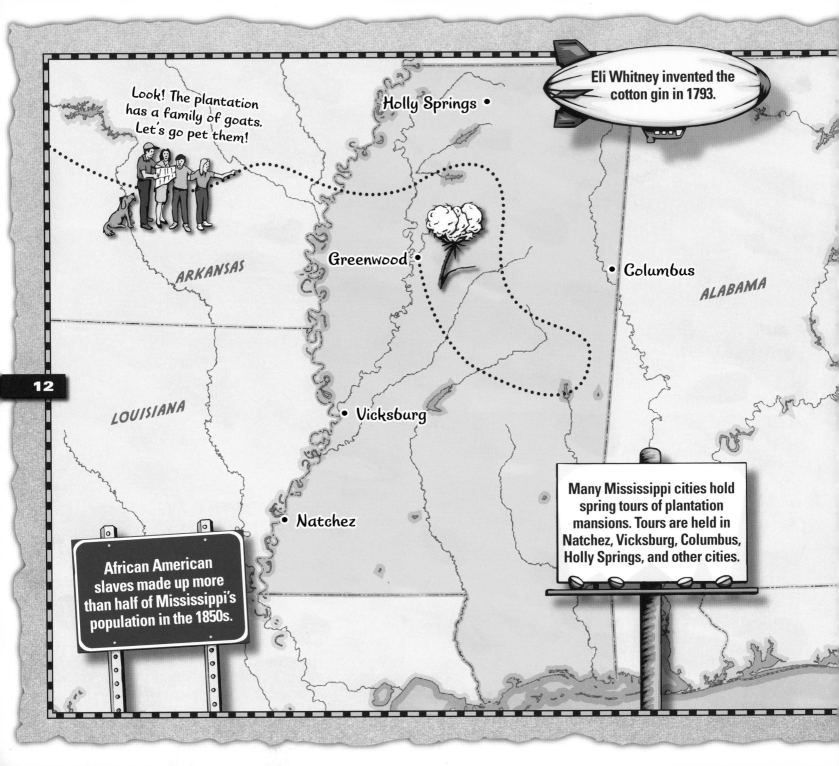

Look! The plantation has a family of goats. Let's go pet them!

Holly Springs

Eli Whitney invented the cotton gin in 1793.

ARKANSAS

Greenwood

Columbus

ALABAMA

12

LOUISIANA

Vicksburg

Many Mississippi cities hold spring tours of plantation mansions. Tours are held in Natchez, Vicksburg, Columbus, Holly Springs, and other cities.

Natchez

African American slaves made up more than half of Mississippi's population in the 1850s.

Walk through the **plantation** owner's home. Then stroll around the grounds. You'll pass barns, sheds, and workshops. And you'll see an old cotton gin. This machine removed seeds from the fluffy cotton. You can even pick your own cotton!

You're touring Florewood River Plantation near Greenwood. Cotton was grown there in the early 1850s. Dozens of African American slaves worked the fields.

Mississippi became an important cotton-growing state. Plantation owners had huge cotton farms. Slaves worked long hours on the farms without pay. They lived in small cabins. The plantation owners' homes were beautiful **mansions.**

Feeling sleepy? This bedroom is part of the Florewood River Plantation.

13

Mississippi was the 20th state to enter the Union. It joined on December 10, 1817.

Ready, aim, fire! Check out the cannons at Vicksburg National Military Park.

Tupelo National Battlefield was the site of a Civil War battle on July 13–15, 1864.

Vicksburg National Military Park

How do you fire an 1800s cannon? Just visit Vicksburg National Military Park. Cannon demonstrations there teach you how it's done.

This site was a battlefield in the Civil War (1861–1865). Northern and Southern states fought this war. The two sides disagreed about slavery. The North opposed slavery. But Southern plantations depended on the slaves' labor. Mississippi and other Southern states left the Union. They formed the Confederate States of America, or Confederacy.

The Union side won the Battle of Vicksburg. After that, the Union controlled the Mississippi River. The Union won the war, too.

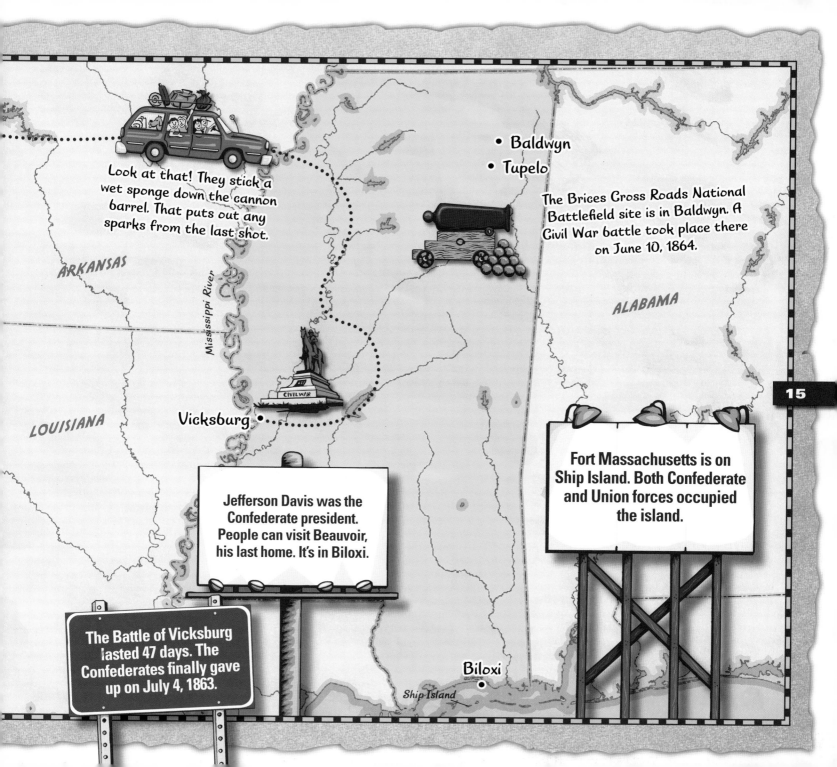

Look at that! They stick a wet sponge down the cannon barrel. That puts out any sparks from the last shot.

ARKANSAS

Mississippi River

LOUISIANA

CIVIL WAR

Vicksburg

• Baldwyn

• Tupelo

The Brices Cross Roads National Battlefield site is in Baldwyn. A Civil War battle took place there on June 10, 1864.

ALABAMA

Fort Massachusetts is on Ship Island. Both Confederate and Union forces occupied the island.

Jefferson Davis was the Confederate president. People can visit Beauvoir, his last home. It's in Biloxi.

The Battle of Vicksburg lasted 47 days. The Confederates finally gave up on July 4, 1863.

Biloxi

Ship Island

ARKANSAS

Those blues guys have really cool names! Muddy Waters and Sunnyland Slim, for example.

Clarksdale

Clarksdale is called the Birthplace of the Blues.

ALABAMA

LOUISIANA

Delta blues singer Muddy Waters (1915–1983) grew up in Clarksdale. His real name was McKinley Morganfield.

John Lee Hooker is a famous Delta blues singer. He was born near Clarksdale. His parents were sharecroppers.

The Delta Blues Museum in Clarksdale

Are you sad sometimes? Then you could have the blues. It might help to sing some blues songs. They tell about being sad or lonely.

Blues songs began among African Americans. One blues style is called Delta blues. It developed in the Mississippi Delta Region. Just visit the Delta Blues Museum. You'll learn all about early blues singers.

Blacks had good reasons to sing the blues. After the Civil War, slaves were freed. But many had nowhere to go. They stayed and worked as **sharecroppers.** Still, they stayed poor. They told about their feelings in blues songs.

Are you a Muddy Waters fan? This exhibit is part of the Delta Blues Museum.

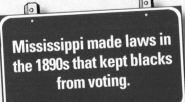

Mississippi made laws in the 1890s that kept blacks from voting.

Ole Miss in Oxford

Ready for college? Don't forget to stop by Ole Miss in Oxford!

The University of Mississippi opened in 1848. Soon it got its nickname—Ole Miss. Ole Miss was in the news in the 1960s. At that time, Mississippi schools were segregated. That is, black and white students were separated. They could not attend the same schools.

In 1962, James Meredith enrolled in Ole Miss. He would be its first African American student. Crowds of people protested, and **riots** broke out. President John F. Kennedy sent National Guard troops to keep order. At last, Meredith could safely begin his classes.

Mississippi suffered many other **civil rights** struggles. By 1969, its schools were open to all students.

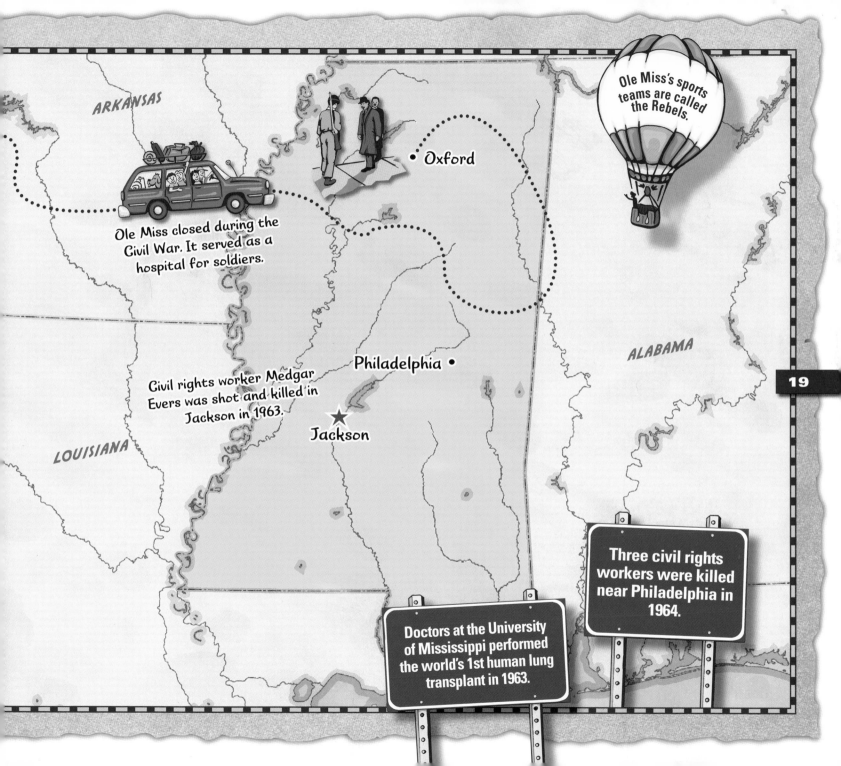

ARKANSAS

Ole Miss closed during the Civil War. It served as a hospital for soldiers.

• Oxford

Ole Miss's sports teams are called the Rebels.

ALABAMA

Philadelphia •

Civil rights worker Medgar Evers was shot and killed in Jackson in 1963.

★ Jackson

LOUISIANA

Three civil rights workers were killed near Philadelphia in 1964.

Doctors at the University of Mississippi performed the world's 1st human lung transplant in 1963.

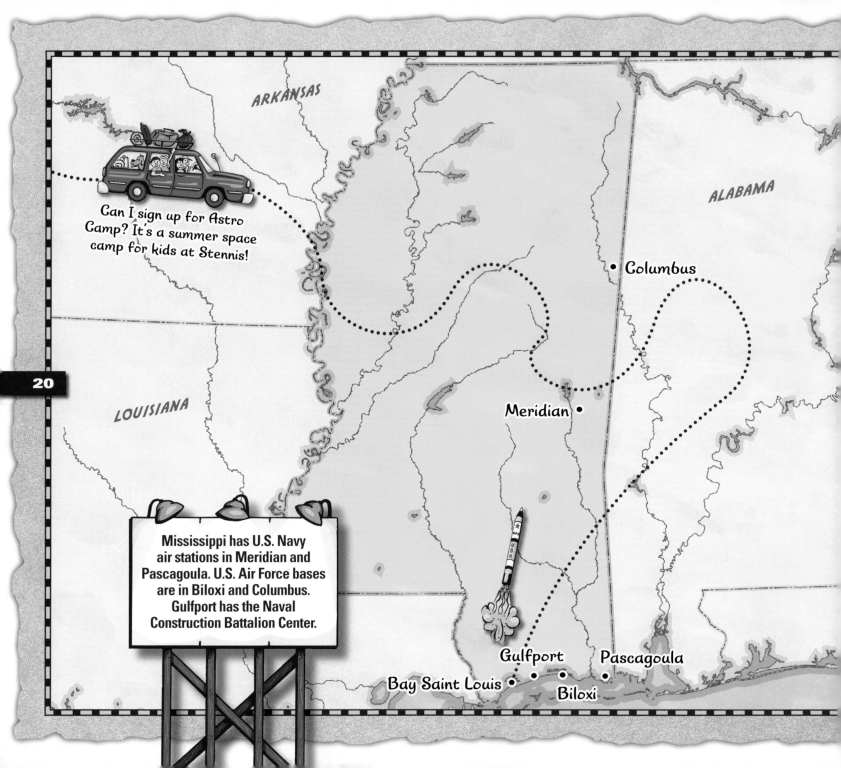

ARKANSAS

ALABAMA

Can I sign up for Astro Camp? It's a summer space camp for kids at Stennis!

• Columbus

LOUISIANA

Meridian •

Mississippi has U.S. Navy air stations in Meridian and Pascagoula. U.S. Air Force bases are in Biloxi and Columbus. Gulfport has the Naval Construction Battalion Center.

Gulfport

Pascagoula

Bay Saint Louis •

Biloxi

Go ahead and take the pilot's seat. Then try landing a space shuttle. Or travel to Mars. Or climb aboard the International Space Station. You're visiting StennisSphere!

StennisSphere is part of Stennis Space Center. This space center is near Bay Saint Louis. It tests rockets and space shuttle engines. It's one of Mississippi's many modern **industries.**

Mississippi factories were busy during World War II (1939–1945). They made war supplies and built ships. Many military bases opened in Mississippi, too. The nation's space program sped up in the 1960s. That's when Stennis Space Center opened.

Would you make a good astronaut? Visit the International Space Station and find out.

21

Ingalls shipyard is in Pascagoula. It builds both military and nonmilitary ships.

22

Mississippi lawmakers work inside the capitol in Jackson.

Mississippi was a territory before it was a state. It became a territory in 1798. Mississippi Territory's 1st capital was Natchez.

Want to see government in action? Just visit the state capitol. That's where Mississippi's state lawmakers work. You can watch them when they're meeting. They talk about laws they want to pass.

Mississippi's state government has three branches. The lawmakers make up one branch. They make the state laws. The governor heads another branch. This branch makes sure laws are carried out. Judges make up the third branch. They study the laws. Then they decide if laws have been broken.

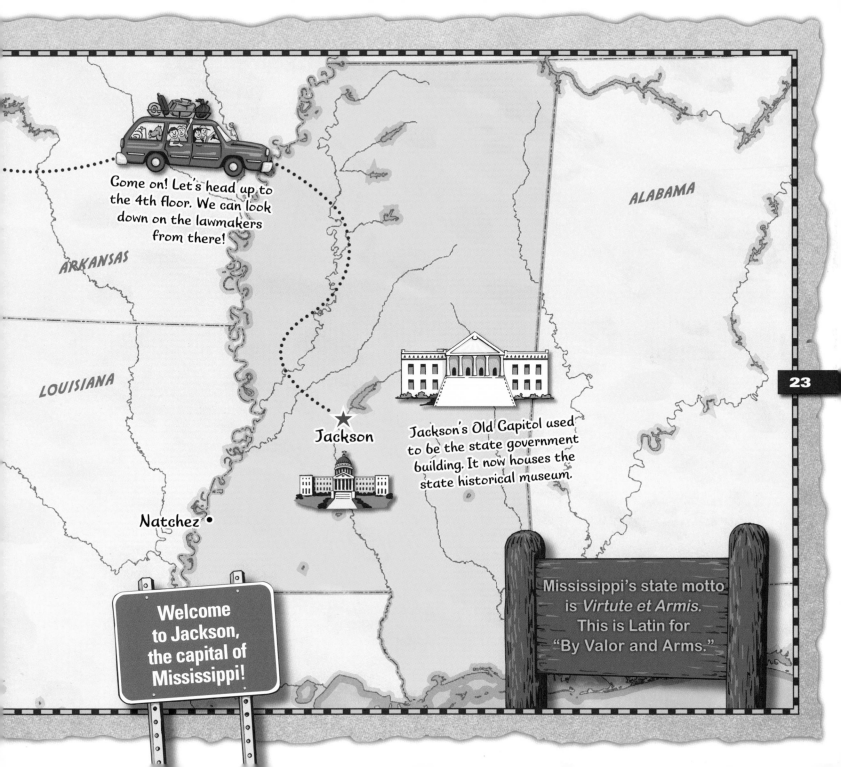

Come on! Let's head up to the 4th floor. We can look down on the lawmakers from there!

ARKANSAS

ALABAMA

LOUISIANA

Jackson

Jackson's Old Capitol used to be the state government building. It now houses the state historical museum.

Natchez •

Welcome to Jackson, the capital of Mississippi!

Mississippi's state motto is *Virtute et Armis*. This is Latin for "By Valor and Arms."

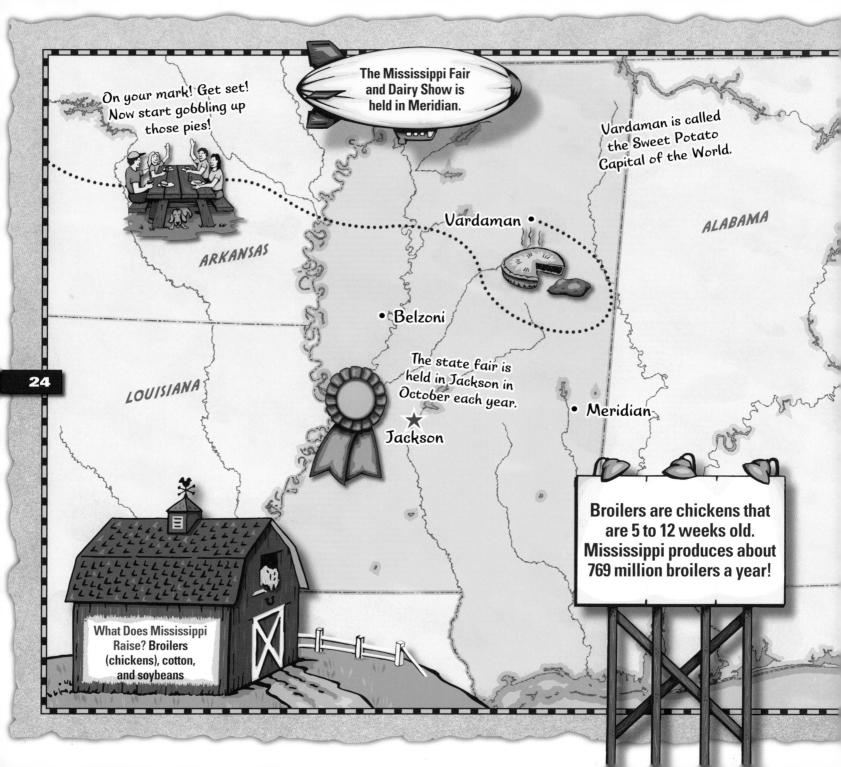

The Mississippi Fair and Dairy Show is held in Meridian.
On your mark! Get set! Now start gobbling up those pies!
Vardaman is called the Sweet Potato Capital of the World.
Vardaman
ALABAMA
ARKANSAS
Belzoni
The state fair is held in Jackson in October each year.
LOUISIANA
Meridian
Jackson
Broilers are chickens that are 5 to 12 weeks old. Mississippi produces about 769 million broilers a year!
What Does Mississippi Raise? Broilers (chickens), cotton, and soybeans

Vardaman's Sweet Potato Festival

Have you ever had sweet potato pie? It's delicious! There are lots of people who love it. They head for Vardaman's Sweet Potato Festival. Why? To enter the sweet potato pie-eating contest!

This festival celebrates a yummy Mississippi crop. Chickens are the state's top farm product. Cotton and soybeans are important field crops.

Forest trees are not exactly crops. But, lumber from trees is very valuable. Mississippi has thousands of tree farms.

Catfish don't seem like farm animals, do they? But Mississippi's fish farmers raise tons of catfish. Most catfish farms are in the Delta Region.

Do you own cotton clothes? These crops might help add to your wardrobe one day!

Mississippi is the top catfish-producing state. Belzoni holds the World Catfish Festival in April.

The Blessing of the Fleet

Fishers work on a shrimp boat offshore near Biloxi.

Shrimp fishing is a big industry in Mississippi. Shrimp fishers work long and hard. They spend hours out in their boats. There are always dangers, too. Storms can blow in quickly. Boats could turn over or spring a leak.

Because of these dangers, Biloxi holds a special event. It takes place at the Biloxi Shrimp Festival. First, a **wreath** is thrown into the water. This honors people lost at sea. Then colorfully decorated shrimp boats line up. A priest blesses them, one by one.

This ceremony is the Blessing of the Fleet. Hundreds of people come to see it. Why not join them?

Biloxi holds an oyster festival every April.

Look over there! They're crowning the Shrimp King and Queen!

Mississippi's oystermen set a record in the winter of 1884–1885. They hauled in 15 million bushels of oysters.

Gulfport's Crawfish Festival takes place in April.

ARKANSAS

LOUISIANA

ALABAMA

Immigrants from many countries live along the coast and work in the seafood industry.

The Maritime and Seafood Industry Museum is in Biloxi.

The shrimp fishing season opens in May. That's when the Biloxi Shrimp Festival takes place.

Biloxi

Gulfport

What Are Mississippi's Fishing Products? Shrimp, oysters, and catfish

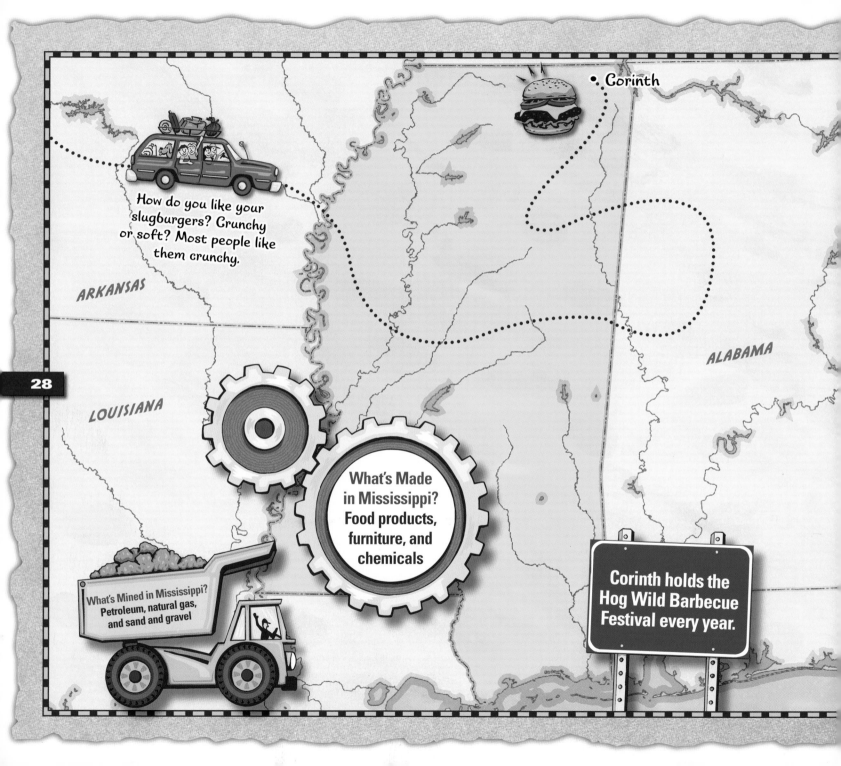

How do you like your slugburgers? Crunchy or soft? Most people like them crunchy.

ARKANSAS

LOUISIANA

ALABAMA

• Corinth

What's Made in Mississippi? Food products, furniture, and chemicals

What's Mined in Mississippi? Petroleum, natural gas, and sand and gravel

Corinth holds the Hog Wild Barbecue Festival every year.

The SlugBurger Festival in Corinth

C ome on by the SlugBurger Festival. You'll love those juicy slugburgers!

Slugs are like snails with no shells. But don't worry. There are no slugs in slugburgers! They're made of beef and soybean meal.

Mississippians are good at making foods. In fact, foods are their major factory products. Many food plants package beef and chicken. Others make spices, drinks, and baked goods.

Mississippi makes lots of wood products, too. The wood comes from the state's forestlands. Pine is the most valuable wood. It's made into furniture and other wood products.

Beef cattle are an important farm product in Mississippi.

Most Mississippi jobs used to be in agriculture. Beginning in 1965, more people worked in manufacturing than in agriculture.

In the mood for rock and roll? Tour Tupelo to learn more about the King!

Have you heard of Elvis Presley? He was called the King of Rock and Roll.

Presley's birthplace is in Tupelo. The house where he was born has a door on each end. It's called a shotgun house. That's because someone could shoot straight through it. They'd shoot in one door and out the other!

Another old-time house was the dog-trot house. It had two big rooms. An open-air hall connected them. Outdoor dogs could trot through that hall!

These house styles were common in rural areas. Those are areas outside of cities and towns. Even today, much of Mississippi is rural. About half the people live in rural areas.

30

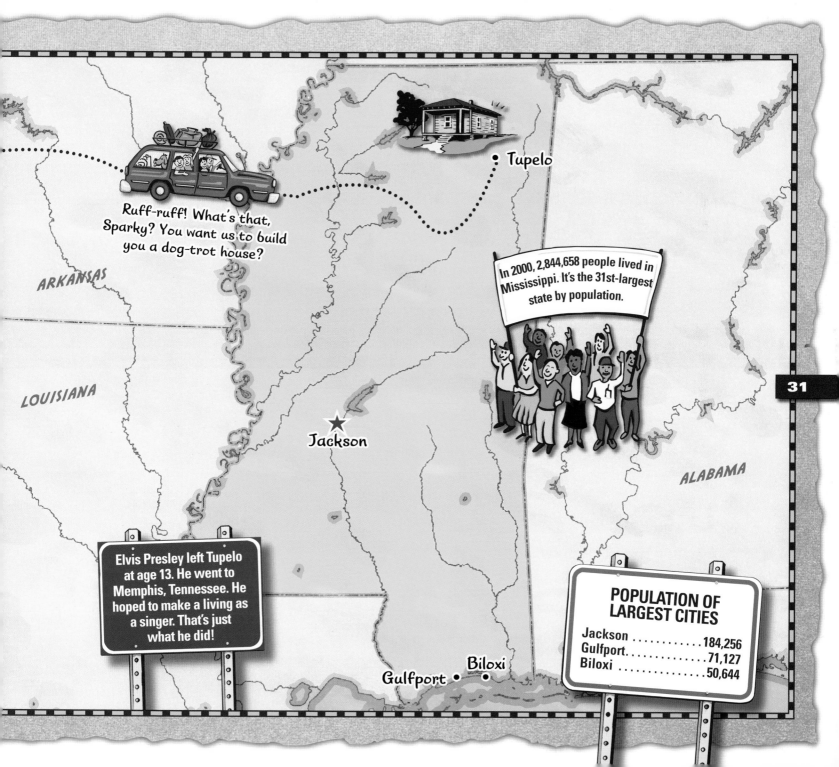

Ruff-ruff! What's that, Sparky? You want us to build you a dog-trot house?

ARKANSAS

LOUISIANA

Tupelo

In 2000, 2,844,658 people lived in Mississippi. It's the 31st-largest state by population.

Jackson

ALABAMA

Elvis Presley left Tupelo at age 13. He went to Memphis, Tennessee. He hoped to make a living as a singer. That's just what he did!

Gulfport • • Biloxi

POPULATION OF LARGEST CITIES

Jackson 184,256
Gulfport. 71,127
Biloxi 50,644

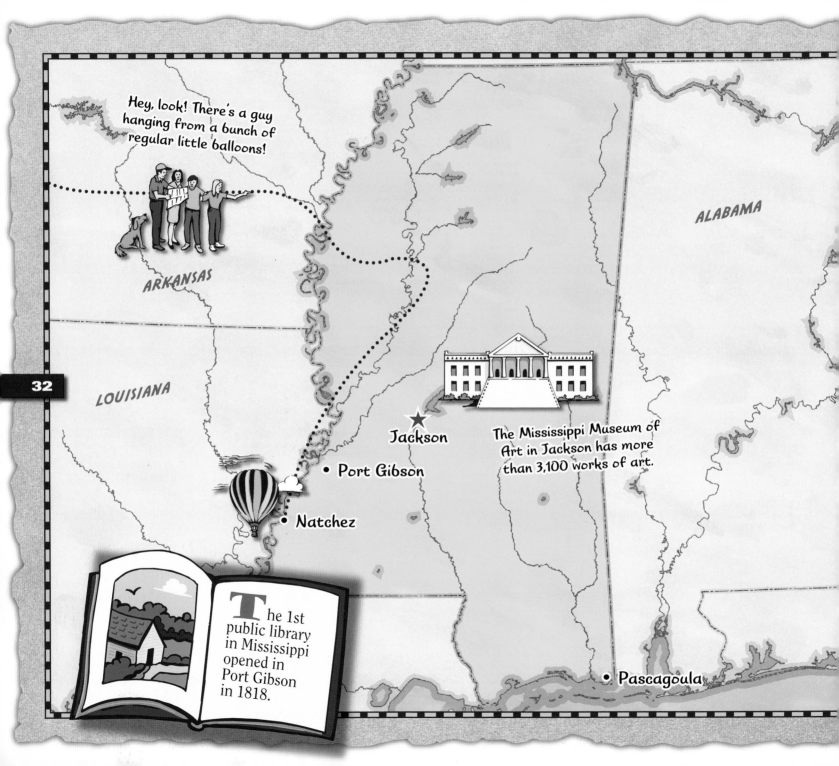

Hey, look! There's a guy hanging from a bunch of regular little balloons!

ALABAMA

ARKANSAS

LOUISIANA

★ Jackson

• Port Gibson

The Mississippi Museum of Art in Jackson has more than 3,100 works of art.

• Natchez

The 1st public library in Mississippi opened in Port Gibson in 1818.

• Pascagoula

The Great Mississippi River Balloon Race

Up, up, and away! Hot-air balloons fill the sky above Natchez.

Hot-air balloons drift through the sky. Many of them have big, colorful stripes. They seem to be moving slowly. But they're racing. It's the Great Mississippi River Balloon Race!

This event takes place in Natchez every October. It's one of Mississippi's many colorful festivals. Some cities celebrate Mardi Gras. It's a carnival with parades and wild costumes.

There's always something fun to do in Mississippi. Many people go to the coast for vacation. Some like to tour plantations and mansions. Others visit museums and historic sites. Nature lovers go wandering through the woods. They enjoy peace and quiet for a change!

Natchez, Pascagoula, and several Gulf Coast towns celebrate Mardi Gras. French settlers brought this festival to the area.

Who wants a horse when you can ride a giraffe? Hop aboard the carousel in Meridian!

Stroll around Meridian. You're in for some big surprises! Turn a corner, and there's a **carousel** horse. Walk through a park, and there's another horse. You'll find them all over town! There are more than forty horses in all. Each one is decorated with colorful designs.

Carousels are a big deal in Meridian. The city's Highland Park has a famous carousel. It started turning around in 1909. And it has more than horses. It has tigers, lions, goats, and giraffes, too! Which one would you like to ride?

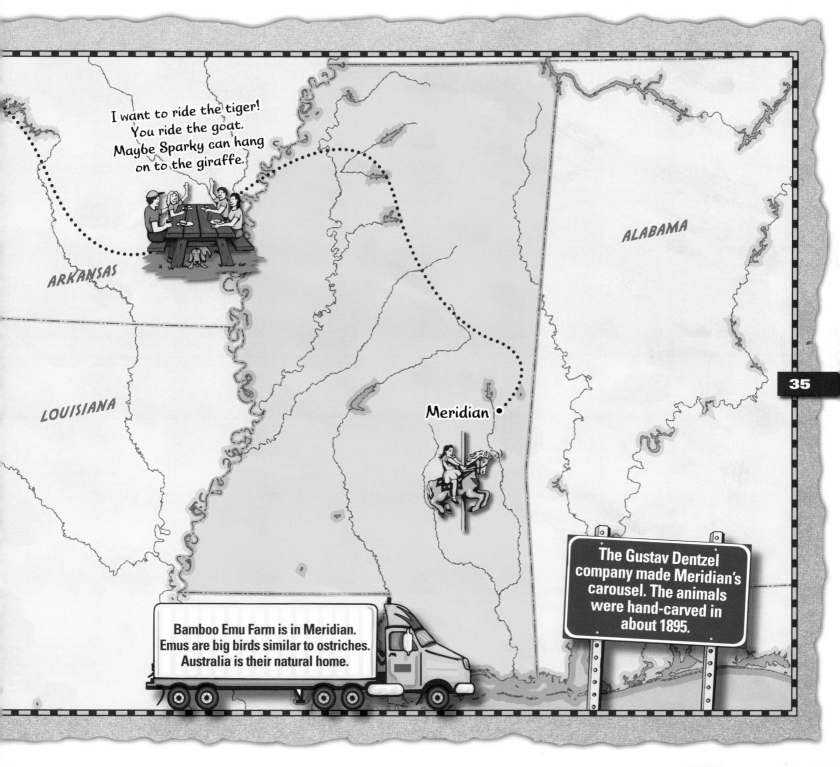

I want to ride the tiger! You ride the goat. Maybe Sparky can hang on to the giraffe.

ARKANSAS

LOUISIANA

ALABAMA

Meridian

The Gustav Dentzel company made Meridian's carousel. The animals were hand-carved in about 1895.

Bamboo Emu Farm is in Meridian. Emus are big birds similar to ostriches. Australia is their natural home.

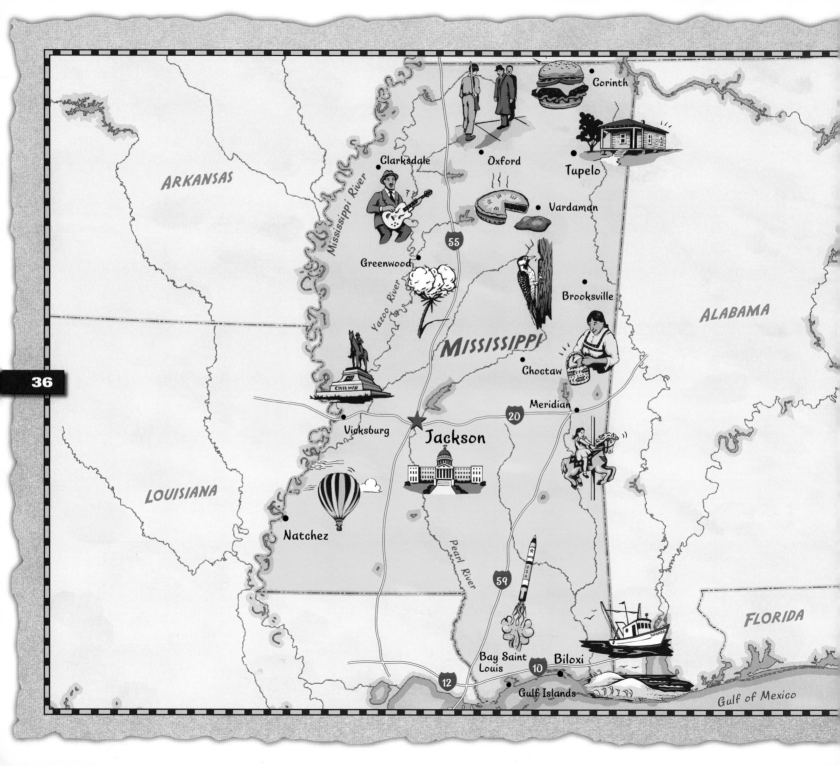

ARKANSAS

Corinth

Clarksdale

Oxford

Tupelo

Mississippi River

Vardaman

Greenwood

Brooksville

ALABAMA

Yazoo River

MISSISSIPPI

CIVIL WAR

Choctaw

Meridian

20

Vicksburg

Jackson

LOUISIANA

Natchez

Pearl River

59

FLORIDA

Bay Saint
Louis

Biloxi

10

12

Gulf Islands

Gulf of Mexico

55

36

OUR TRIP

We visited many amazing places on our trip! We also met a lot of interesting people along the way. Look at the map on the left. Use your finger to trace all the places we have been.

How old are the trees in the Petrified Forest? See page 7 for the answer.

What grows in Cypress Swamp? Page 9 has the answer.

Who invented the cotton gin? See page 12 for the answer.

How long did the Battle of Vicksburg last? Look on page 15 for the answer.

What's Astro Camp? Page 20 has the answer.

What is Vardaman called? Turn to page 24 for the answer.

When does the shrimp fishing season open? Look on page 27 and find out!

When did Elvis Presley leave Tupelo? Turn to page 31 for the answer.

That was a great trip! We have traveled all over Mississippi!

There are a few places that we didn't have time for, though. Next time, we plan to visit the Jackson Zoological Park. In March, it hosts the Zoolympics. Kids can participate in events such as the Zebra Kick and the Cheetah Relay!

More Places to Visit in Mississippi

WORDS TO KNOW

carousel (KAIR-uh-sell) a merry-go-round

civil rights (SIV-il RITES) the rights of a nation's citizens, such as voting and education rights

fawns (FAWNZ) baby deer

frybread (FRYE-bred) a deep-fried bread made by American Indians

hominy (HA-muh-nee) corn kernels that are soaked so they swell up

immigrants (IM-uh-gruhntz) people who move to a new country from their home country

industries (IN-duh-streez) types of businesses

legends (LEJ-uhndz) stories created to explain mysteries

mansions (MAN-shuhnz) large, elegant homes

plantation (plan-TAY-shuhn) a large farm that raises mainly 1 crop

riots (RYE-uhts) public disorder by large crowds

sharecroppers (SHAIR-krop-urz) people who rent farmland and pay their rent with crops

wreath (REETH) leaves or flowers woven into a circle

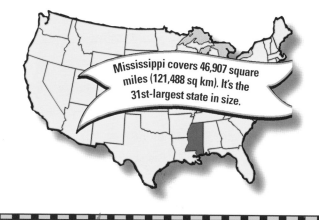

Mississippi covers 46,907 square miles (121,488 sq km). It's the 31st-largest state in size.

STATE SYMBOLS

State beverage: Milk

State bird: Mockingbird

State fish: Largemouth bass (black bass)

State flower: Magnolia

State fossil: Prehistoric whale

State insect: Honeybee

State land mammal: White-tailed deer

State shell: Oyster shell

State stone: Petrified wood

State tree: Magnolia

State waterfowl: Wood duck

State water mammal: Bottle-nosed dolphin (porpoise)

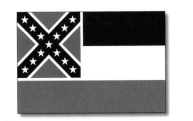

State flag

State seal

STATE SONG

"Go, Mississippi"

Words and music by Houston Davis

States may sing their songs of praise
With waving flags and hip-hoo-rays,
Let cymbals crash and let bells ring
'Cause here's one song I'm proud to sing.

Choruses:
Go, Mississippi, keep rolling along,
Go, Mississippi, you cannot go wrong,
Go, Mississippi, we're singing your song,
M-I-S-S-I-S-S-I-P-P-I.

Go, Mississippi, you're on the right track,
Go, Mississippi, and this is a fact,
Go, Mississippi, you'll never look back,
M-I-S-S-I-S-S-I-P-P-I.

Go, Mississippi, straight down the line,
Go, Mississippi, ev'rything's fine,
Go, Mississippi, it's your state and mine,
M-I-S-S-I-S-S-I-P-P-I.

Go, Mississippi, continue to roll,
Go, Mississippi, the top is the goal,
Go, Mississippi, you'll have and you'll hold,
M-I-S-S-I-S-S-I-P-P-I.

Go, Mississippi, get up and go,
Go, Mississippi, let the world know,
That our Mississippi is leading the show,
M-I-S-S-I-S-S-I-P-P-I.

FAMOUS PEOPLE

Diddley, Bo (1928–), guitarist

Evers, Charles (1922–), civil rights leader

Evers, Medgar (1925–1963), civil rights leader

Faulkner, William (1897–1962), author

Favre, Brett (1969–), football player

Freeman, Morgan (1937–), actor

Henson, Jim (1936–1990), creator of the Muppets

Hill, Faith (1967–), singer

Jones, James Earl (1931–), actor

King, B. B. (1925–), blues musician

Payton, Walter (1954–1999), football player

Presley, Elvis (1935–1977), singer

Revels, Hiram Rhoades (1822–1901), 1st African American elected to U.S. Senate

Taylor, Mildred D. (1943–), children's author

Waters, Muddy (1915–1983), blues musician

Wells-Barnett, Ida B. (1862–1931), journalist, civil rights leader

Welty, Eudora (1909–2001), author

Williams, Tennessee (1911–1983), playwright

Winfrey, Oprah (1954–), talk show host

Wynette, Tammy (1942–1998), singer

TO FIND OUT MORE

At the Library

Gourse, Leslie. *Jim Henson, Young Puppeteer*. New York: Aladdin Paperbacks, 2000.

Moore, Heidi. *Ida B. Wells-Barnett*. Chicago: Heinemann Library, 2004.

Shoulders, Michael, and Rick Anderson (illustrator). *M Is for Magnolia: A Mississippi Alphabet*. Chelsea, Mich.: Sleeping Bear Press, 2003.

Siebert, Diane, and Greg Harlin (illustrator). *Mississippi*. New York: HarperCollins Publishers, 2001.

Wiles, Deborah, and Jerome Lagarrigue (illustrator). *Freedom Summer*. New York: Atheneum Books for Young Readers, 2001.

On the Web

Visit our home page for lots of links about Mississippi:
http://www.childsworld.com/links

Note to Parents, Teachers, and Librarians: We routinely verify our Web links to make sure they are safe, active sites—so encourage your readers to check them out!

Places to Visit or Contact

Mississippi Development Authority
Division of Tourism Development
PO Box 849
Jackson, MS 39205
601/359-3297
For more information about traveling in Mississippi

The Old Capitol Museum of Mississippi History
PO Box 571
Jackson, MS 39205-0571
601/576-6920
For more information about the history of Mississippi

INDEX

Bye, Magnolia State.
We had a great time.
We'll come back soon!